Ancient Greece

Author   Mary Jo Keller
Illustrator   Linda Milliken

EP062 ©Highsmith® Inc. 1995, 2002, 2007
W5527 State Road 106, P.O. Box 800
Fort Atkinson, WI 53538

Table of Contents

The Hands-on Heritage series has been designed to help you bring culture to life in your classroom! Look for the "For the Teacher" headings to find information to help you prepare for activities. Simply block out these sections when reproducing pages for student use.

Ancient Greek World

European civilization started in Greece more than 2,000 years ago. In those days, Greece controlled most of the land bordering the Mediterranean and Black seas.

To the Greeks of the fifth century B.C., the world consisted of the Mediterranean Sea and the land around it. Herodotus was the first Greek historian. He was known as "The Father of History." He traveled throughout the civilized world in the mid-400s B.C. recording what he learned about the religions, customs, and cultures of other civilizations.

The Greeks believed the Mediterranean Sea stretched westward to the gardens of the Hesperides. This is where the sun god, Helios, landed his golden chariot every evening. He was born in a golden cup in his palace in the east. The next morning he drove his fiery chariot across the sky, giving light to gods and mortals all day.

Project
Make a map and learn about modern map-making.

Materials
- map of ancient world (below)
- modern map of the world
- neighborhood map (available in the phone book or from a real estate broker)
- paper
- pencils

Directions
1. Compare the map of the ancient world to a map of the world as it currently exists.
2. Draw a map of what you think your neighborhood looks like. Compare your drawing to an actual map of the area.
3. Discuss the equipment modern map makers use to make their work so accurate (i.e. satellites and computers).

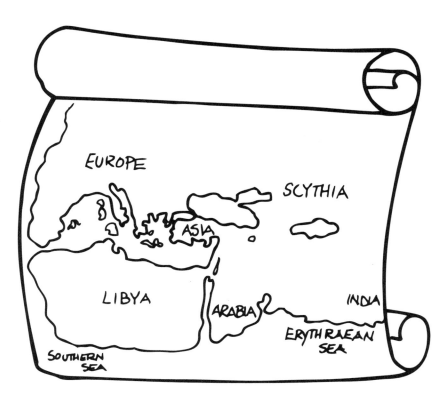

Time Line

The Minoan culture was the first major civilization in the Greek world. It arose on the island of Crete about 3000 B.C. The development of Greek civilization began about 2000 B.C., when small farming villages were founded in Greece. This culture, called the Mycenaean culture, prospered on the Greek mainland from about 1600 to 1200 B.C. Greece's Dark Age lasted from about 1100 to 800 B.C. In 776 B.C., the first Olympic games took place. In 490 and 479 B.C., the Greeks twice defeated Persian armies. The greatest art was produced during the Golden Age of Athens, 461 to 431 B.C. Sparta defeated Athens in the Peloponnesian War that lasted from 431 to 404 B.C. In 338 B.C., Philip II of Macedonia conquered the Greeks. Alexander the Great conquered most of the territory from Egypt to India in the years from 334 to 328 B.C. He built Greek cities and introduced the Greek culture wherever he ruled. In 323 B.C., Alexander the Great died and the Hellenistic age began. In 197 B.C., Greece found itself defeated by the Romans for the first time. But the Greeks kept fighting back, and the Romans continued to return. It wasn't until 146 B.C. that Greece was finally conquered by the Romans.

Project
Chart and illustrate the history of the ancient Greek empire.

Materials
- white butcher paper
- pencils, markers, or crayons
- ruler

Directions
1. Cut a long length of butcher paper.
2. Draw a line lengthwise across the middle of the paper. Mark the year 30 B.C. to the far right on the line. Using the information above, mark the other important years in Greece's early history.
3. Illustrate the events beneath the time line.

For the Teacher
Explain the term "B.C."

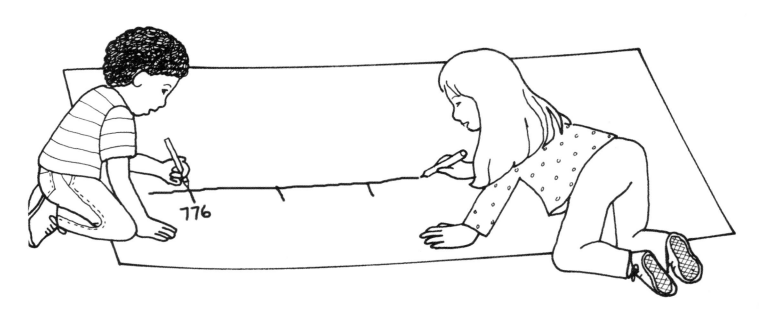

Democracy in Athens

The government of the city of Athens was a democracy—the people held the ruling power. However, the only people considered full citizens were men who were born there. The citizens met in a single assembly called the *ecclesia*. It was at these meetings that the people voted for laws and directed the magistrates who were chosen by lot to govern the city. If a magistrate did a poor job, he could be banished from the city for 10 years! This procedure was called *ostracism,* and we still use the same word today to mean banishment.

Any citizen had the right to speak in the ecclesia. The speaker would place a wreath of myrtle on his head. He was allowed a certain amount of time in which to speak. His time was measured by a *clepsydra* or water clock. He had to finish speaking before all the water from one *amphora* (pottery jar) ran into another.

Project
Make a water clock. Use the water clock to keep time for a short speech.

Materials
- two large, empty cans of the same size
- clock or watch with second hand
- can opener
- water

Directions
1. Make a small opening on the bottom edge of one can as illustrated.
2. Arrange the cans on a step or box so that the can with the hole is above the other can. Add water to the top can. Time how long it takes for the top can to empty. The time can be adjusted by adding or draining some water.

3. Pretend your class is a group of citizens at an ecclesia. Take turns speaking about "What I Remember Most About Ancient Greece" until the water clock runs out. To "reset" for the next student, simply pour the water from the bottom can back into the top can.

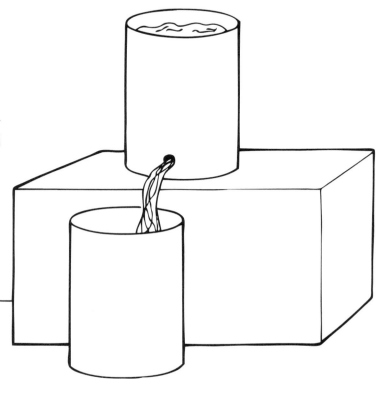

Warships

The Greeks were excellent shipbuilders. They built trading ships and ships to protect their long coastline from attack. Athens was the main naval power, and many warships were built at her docks.

An example of a fast warship is the *trireme* (trī´ rēm). The fronts of these boats were made to look like sea monsters, with a magic eye to ward off bad luck. Attached to the front of the boat was a sharp metal spike that was used as a ram to pierce the side of an enemy ship. Scores of oarsmen sat in three tiers on each side of the ship. Their oars were different lengths depending on the height of the rower's seat. The rowers on the top level had to pull an oar that was 10 feet long! Sometimes two men worked a single oar. The men rowed in time to flute music. In a battle, these strong men would row very fast to build up speed, pull in their oars and break off the oars of the enemy ship as they sailed past.

Project

Design the prow of a Greek trireme. Create a scenic picture of a trireme sailing on the Mediterranean Sea.

Materials

- blue and green tissue paper
- white construction paper
- starch
- paintbrush
- Trireme Pattern
- scissors
- crayons or colored pencils
- research materials

Directions

1. Tear the tissue paper into narrow strips. Lay them across the paper and brush down with starch. Mix some green strips with the blues to look like sea water.

2. Color, cut out, and tape together the two halves of the warship. Don't forget to draw the magic eye on the front of the ship. Glue to the sea to complete your picture.

3. Research to find out when triremes were best used in warfare. In what situations were they most effective? What would the modern-day equivalent of a trireme be? Write a paragraph detailing your research and attach it to the bottom of your picture.

For the Teacher

Make a copy of the Trireme Pattern for each student.

EP062 Ancient Greece © Highsmith® Inc. 2007

Trireme Pattern

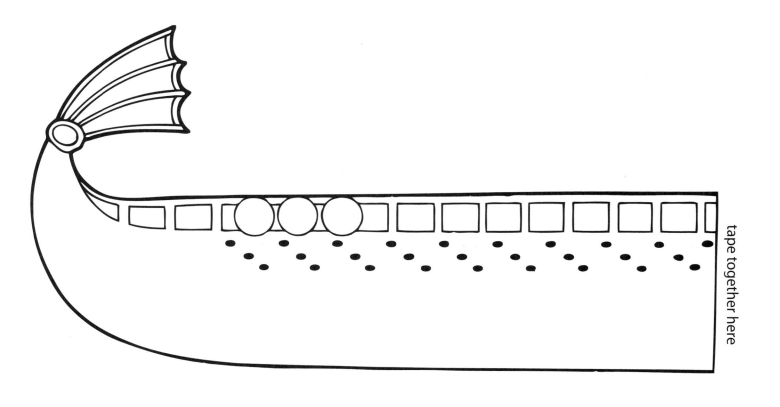

tape together here

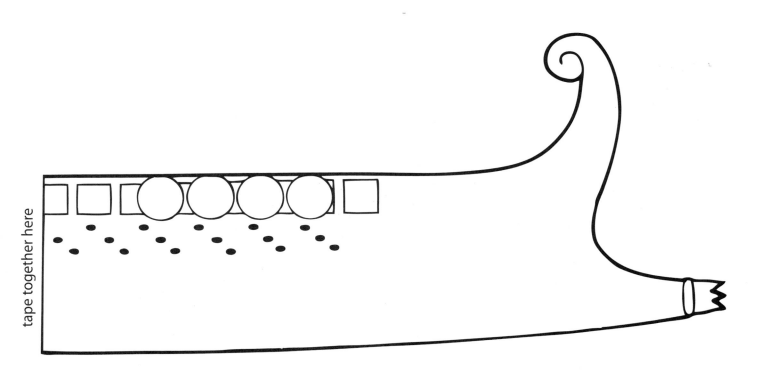

tape together here

Agora

Ancient Greece was divided into very small independent states that consisted of a town and the surrounding farmland. These were called *city-states*. There was an open space at the center of each town called the *agora*. The word agora originally meant "meeting." The word came to mean "town center" because the men gathered there to discuss the important matters of the city-state.

The agora was surrounded by the main buildings of the city such as the law courts, army headquarters, and the mint. The area was also used as the marketplace and was always crowded with shoppers and merchants. Farmers, bakers, cheese makers, and fishermen displayed their wares in market stalls. Slaves could be purchased on a special day each month. Nearby were the workshops where many goods, such as pots, sandals, and jewelry, were made.

For the Teacher

Project
Recreate an ancient Greek marketplace in the classroom.

Materials
- large towels or blankets
- articles to "sell" from Agora Project Page
- shopping baskets
- bracelets (page 36) for jewelers to sell
- pita bread for bakers to sell

Directions
1. The class can make items for the market. Reproduce and cut apart several Agora Project Pages. Give a project to each student to make.

2. Have students bring a basket from home to hold their purchases. There were no paper bags available at the agora!

2. On market day, push the desks aside to create the marketplace. Some vendors had stalls to sell from, others spread out blankets. Use desks covered with blankets for stalls, or spread out blankets or towels on the floor.

3. Divide students into farmers, potters, metal workers, traders, bakers, jewelers, and sandal makers. Have them take turns shopping and minding their wares.

Agora Project Page

Potter

Greek lamps looked like Aladdin's lamp, but they sometimes had two or more spouts.

Materials: clay, water

Directions

1. Roll clay into a ball half the size of a tennis ball. Push your thumbs into clay, pinching and pressing clay into a lamp shape.
2. Make two clay coils. Form one into a circle for the lamp's base. Make a handle from the other coil. Attach these coils by moistening them with a little bit of water.

Sandal Maker

Athenian women had their sandals custom made from wooden soles and soft leather.

Materials: heavy cardboard, pencil, scissors, fabric strips, hole punch

Directions

1. Trace the outline of your customer's foot onto the cardboard. Cut out. Punch holes in the sole as shown.
2. Cut fabric into three strips 3 x 36 inches (7.6 x 90 cm). Lace one piece of fabric through the holes as if lacing a sneaker. Attach the remaining pieces by tying them to the ends of the first piece. To wear, place foot under the laced part. Wrap strips around the leg to the knee and tie.

Farmer

Barley is unfamiliar to many people today, but it was a staple in the Greek diet.

Materials: nuts, carrots, grapes, dates, cheese, barley, celery, baskets, or terra cotta pots

Directions

1. Arrange food in baskets or in pots.
2. After "shopping," celery, carrots and barley can be used in recipes on page 46.

Merchants

Traders imported items such as wheat, wood, mineral ores and refined metals, silks, and fabric dyes from around the known world to sell at the agora. Make imported "silk" headbands to sell.

Materials: fabric, scissors, crayons

Directions

1. Cut the fabric into lengths about 2 x 36 inches (5 x 90 cm).
2. Decorate with a Greek "key" design.

Metalworkers

Craftsmen fashioned the pins that were used to fasten the Greeks' garments.

Materials: tagboard, scissors, toothpicks, aluminum foil, safety pins or pin backs, hot glue gun or tape

Directions

1. Cut tagboard into circles about 1½ inches (3.8 cm) in diameter. Cover with foil.
2. Gently emboss designs into the foil with a toothpick.
3. Tape a safety pin to back or use hot glue to attach a pin back.

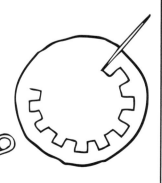

Foot Soldiers

Each Greek city-state had its own army. Sometimes the states fought each other and sometimes they fought together against a foreign enemy. Athens, Sparta, and Thebes had the strongest armies in Greece.

Foot soldiers were called *hoplites* because the Greek word for the round shields they carried was *hoplon*. These soldiers fought with two-edged swords and long wooden spears with metal points. Their armor consisted of a bronze breastplate, a helmet, and "greaves" made of metal or leather to protect the soldier's legs. Sometimes a fringed leather apron was worn for further protection of the torso. Hoplites fought in a block or phalanx formation, consisting of about eight lines of soldiers. They all moved in step to the music of a pipe. If the soldiers broke rank, the group became vulnerable.

Project
Make a "leather apron" similar to the ones used by the hoplites on their shields.

Materials
- large paper bags (grocery bags)
- crayons
- scissors
- water

Directions
1. Cut down the seam of the paper bag and cut off the bottom. Crush and crumple the bag, Dip it in water, then smooth it out to dry.
2. When dry, cut the bag into an apron shape as shown, remembering to include the fringe.
3. Color with crayons. A popular design used in ancient Greek times was one large eye.

EP062 Ancient Greece © Highsmith® Inc. 2007

Coins

Before the seventh century B.C., the Greeks did not use money. Instead, they used a system of barter, exchanging goods instead of buying them. The earliest money was an iron spit or skewer called an *obol*. Over time, these small rods were replaced with coins. The first coins were made in silver, but later coins were minted in gold.

The ore to make the coins was extracted from deep underground mines. Since this was difficult and dangerous work, most of the miners were slaves. The ore was refined by metal smelters and smiths before being sent to be minted. The coins, called *drachmas*, were made by placing a piece of metal on an anvil between two molds. The worker made the coin by hitting the mold hard with a metal hammer. The edges were trimmed off. Drachmas had a picture of the goddess Athena on one side and her sacred bird on the other side. The word drachma means "bundle of spits."

Project
The first coins minted in mainland Greece were the Aegina tortoises. Make a replica of this early coin.

Materials
- 2 slices stale white bread
- 2 Tbsp. (30 ml) white glue
- black and white poster paint
- newspaper
- toothpick

Directions
1. Remove the crusts from the bread.
2. Tear the bread into pieces and place in a bowl with the glue. Add a few drops of both black and white paint to make the bread silver colored. Knead until no longer sticky.
3. Form mixture so that it resembles a coin. Add details of a tortoise and its shell with a toothpick. Let dry.

Language

The Greek language was in use for centuries before written records were kept. Prehistoric people who migrated to Greece from Asia developed different dialects. Because Athens became the center of art and politics, the language used there became the chief language used throughout ancient Greece.

This ancient Greek language differs in several ways from the language spoken in Greece today, but the printed alphabet is almost unchanged from the ancient letters.

Many of the words we use in English are borrowed from the Greek. Artists, scientists, and doctors might be surprised to learn how much Greek they know!

Project
Learn a few words in the ancient Greek language.

Materials
- card stock
- Greek Words Project Page
- colored pencils
- scissors

Directions
1. Color and cut apart the cards. Each card provides the Greek spelling in all capital letters and the pronunciation.
2. Write the English word for the picture on the back of the card.
3. Practice memorizing the words with the help of these flashcards. Practice with a friend!

For the Teacher
1. Reproduce the Greek Words Project Page (13) on card stock.
2. For answers, refer to the key below.

Answer Key
1. mother	7. large
2. tree	8. day
3. book	9. father
4. earth	10. world
5. small	11. friend
6. house	12. letter

EP062 Ancient Greece © Highsmith® Inc. 2007

Greek Words Project Page

1. ΜΗΤΗΡ — MAY tayr

2. ΔΕΝΔΡΟΝ — DEHN drohn

3. ΒΙΒΛΙΟΝ — bihb LEE ohn

4. ΓΗ — gay

5. ΜΙΚΡΟΣ — mee KROHS

6. ΟΙΚΙΑ — oy KEE ah

7. ΜΕΓΑΣ — MEH gahs

8. ΗΜΕΡΑ — hay MEH rah

9. ΓΙΑΤΗΡ — pah TAYR

10. ΚΟΣΜΟΣ — KOHS mohs

11. ΦΙΛΟΣ — FEE lohs

12. ΓΡΑΜΜΑ — GRAHM mah

Alphabet

Our word *alphabet* comes from the names of the first two letters of the Greek alphabet: alpha and beta. Most of the alphabets of modern Europe are based on the Greek alphabet. Greek letters were made of mostly straight lines. This is because most of the writing was done on tablets made of wax. The letters were scratched into the wax with a pointed tool called a *stylus*.

Older writing might be made top to bottom, left to right, or bottom to top. Early Greek scribes wrote left to right until the end of a line and then came back from right to left on the next line. They called this *boustrophedon* or "turning like an ox plowing a field." Later, Greeks decided to write from the left to the right as we still do today. Words were written with no space between them and no punctuation!

Project
Practice writing the letters of the Greek alphabet. Write a message for a friend to decode using capital English letters.

Materials
- copy of Greek Alphabet chart
- pencil
- paper

Directions
1. Practice copying the letters of the Greek alphabet.
2. Write a message in the style of the ancient Greek scribes. Write in capital English letters. Start at the bottom right corner of the paper and write to the left. On the next line, write left to right. Do not leave spaces between the words and do not use any punctuation. Trade messages with a friend and see how long it takes to decode.

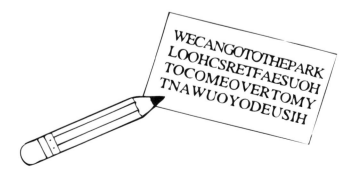

For the Teacher
Copy the Greek Alphabet chart for each student or copy the alphabet to the chalkboard.

The Greek Alphabet

A	alpha	N	nu
B	beta	Ξ	xi
Γ	gamma	O	omicron
Δ	delta	Π	pi
E	epsilon	P	rho
Z	zeta	Σ	sigma
H	eta	T	tau
Θ	theta	Υ	uppsilon
I	iota	Φ	phi
K	kappa	X	chi
Λ	lambda	Ψ	psi
M	mu	Ω	omega

Education

A boy growing up in Sparta would have a very different kind of education than his counterpart in Athens. In Sparta, physical fitness was more important than anything. In their state boarding schools, boys learned endurance, discipline, and obedience. They became excellent soldiers.

Every boy in Athens had to learn a trade, but there were no laws about school. If a family could afford private school, their sons would learn to read, write, count with an abacus, play a stringed instrument called a *lyre*, and recite poetry. Students spent the afternoons exercising in the gymnasium. Older boys either became apprentices or studied with professional teachers called *Sophists*.

Project
Make an abacus and practice showing numbers.

Materials
- brass brads
- shoebox lid
- scissors

Directions
1. Carefully cut four slits in the box lid.
2. Insert 10 brads into each column. Experiment with showing different numbers on the abacus and see if your friends can decipher them.

How to use the abacus:
The column on the right is the ones column. Each brad has a value of one. The next column to the left is the tens column. Each brad on this column has a value of 10. The third column to the left is the hundreds column, and each brad has a value of 100. The fourth column to the left is the thousands column. Each brad on this column has a value of 1,000.

Start with all the brads at the bottom, toward you. As you work, push one or more brads to the top, away from you.

Suppose you want to show the number 1,352. Push up one brad in thousands column (1,000); push up three brads in the hundreds column (300); push up five brads in the tens column (50); and push up two brads in the ones column (2).

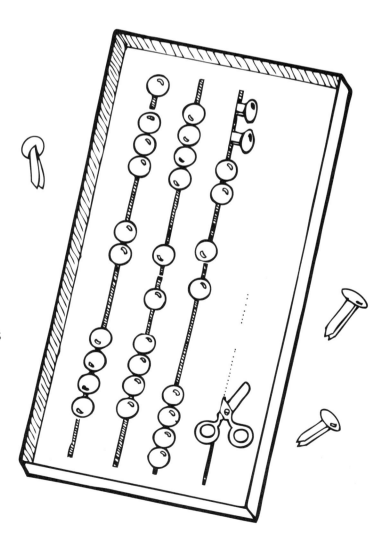

Physical Fitness

Physical fitness was very important to the ancient Greeks. They believed that a fit and healthy body was just as important as an educated mind. Men and boys would spend part of every day at the gymnasium.

In the city-state of Sparta, seven-year-old boys were sent to camp to begin their training to become soldiers and athletes. They were taught physical skills rather than mental ones. At age 11, their training became even harder. The boys were deliberately kept hungry and their only clothing was a thin cloak, even in winter. They would rub themselves with snow and bathe in the icy river.

Sparta was the only city-state where girls and boys were treated equally. The girls were trained to be strong and independent. They learned to throw a discus and javelin, and run a foot race.

Project
Exercise and running were part of the daily life of a Spartan youth. Practice these skills.

Materials
- large field or playground

Directions
1. Warm up by slowly jogging in place for two minutes.
2. Practice doing some jumping jacks, sit-ups, and push-ups.
3. Run around the perimeter of the field or playground.
4. Hold a foot race with two or more classmates. Make sure you have a judge at the finish line in case the race is close!
5. Imagine what it would be like to spend a major part of your day developing your physical skills. Would you enjoy it? Why or why not? Discuss as a class.

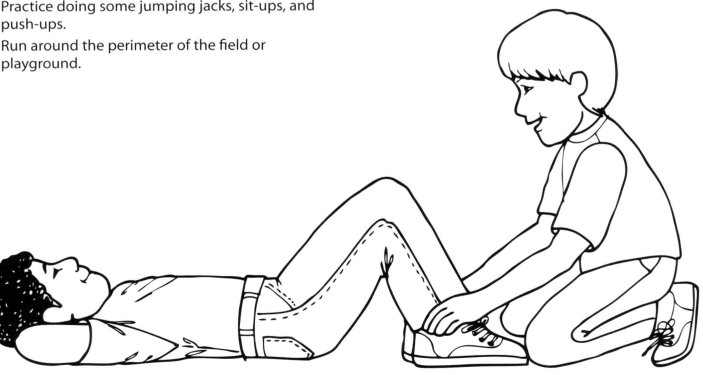

EP062 Ancient Greece © Highsmith® Inc. 2007

Science

Archimedes was one of the greatest mathematicians, engineers, and physicists of ancient times. One of his famous engineering inventions was a water-removing device. This device, called the Archimedean Screw, is still used in Egypt today!

One day, the king of Syracuse asked Archimedes to find out if his crown was made of solid gold or if some silver had been added. Archimedes decided to take a bath and think about the problem. As he lowered himself into the bath, the water rose and spilled over the edge. He shouted, "Eureka! I have found it!" Archimedes discovered that the volume of an object determines the amount of water it will displace. The volume of the water equals the volume of the object. Unfortunately for the goldsmith, Archimedes also learned that the king had been cheated.

Project

Conduct an experiment to test the buoyancy of solids in water.

Materials

- string
- stone
- spring scale
- container of water
- paper and pencil

Directions

1. Weigh the stone on the scale and record its weight.
2. Place the container of water on the scale. Holding the stone by the string, suspend the stone in the water. Record its weight.

3. What is the difference in the weight of the stone in and out of the water? Why is there a difference? What happens to the water when the stone is lowered into it?

Mathematics

Some of the greatest mathematicians and scientists in the ancient world were Greeks. Pythagoras was a mathematician who lived during the sixth century B.C. He formed a community in Italy where students could study philosophy and the relationships between numbers. He developed many mathematical theories including one about the relationship of the sides of a right triangle. Students today still study this proposition, called the *Pythagorean Theorem*.

Euclid, also a mathematician, studied astronomy, geometry, arithmetic, music, and harmony at the Academy in Athens. He was invited by King Ptolemy of Egypt to teach at his famous "Musaeon" or University of Scholars at Alexandria. Here Euclid studied and wrote his *Elements*. It contained 465 geometry propositions and proofs, including the Pythagorean Theorem, and it remains the basis for courses in geometry.

Project

Test some math theories that were proposed by Euclid and Pythagoras.

Materials

- paper
- pencil
- 25 poker chips
- Math Sheet

Directions

1. Try to figure out as many questions on the Math Sheet as you can.

For the Teacher

1. Reproduce one copy of the Math Sheet (page 19) for each student.
2. Allow the students time to try the mathematical questions alone or with a friend.

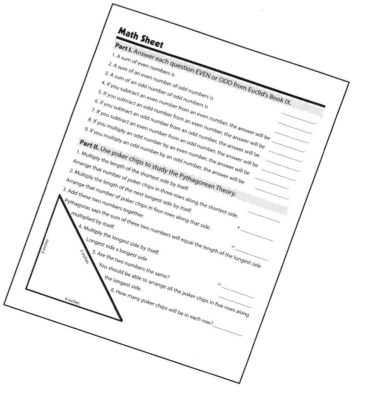

Answer Key

Part I	Part II
1. even	1. 9
2. even	2. 16
3. odd	3. 25
4. even	4. 25
5. odd	5. Yes
6. even	6. 5
7. odd	
8. even	
9. odd	

Math Sheet

Part I. Answer each question EVEN or ODD from Euclid's Book IX.

1. A sum of even numbers is _____.

2. A sum of an even number of odd numbers is _____.

3. A sum of an odd number of odd numbers is _____.

4. If you subtract an even number from an even number, the answer will be _____.

5. If you subtract an odd number from an even number, the answer will be _____.

6. If you subtract an odd number from an odd number, the answer will be _____.

7. If you subtract an even number from an odd number, the answer will be _____.

8. If you multiply an odd number by an even number, the answer will be _____.

9. If you multiply an odd number by an odd number, the answer will be _____.

Part II. Use poker chips to study the Pythagorean Theorem.

1. Multiply the length of the shortest side of the triangle below by itself. _____.

   Arrange that number of poker chips in three rows along the shortest side.

2. Multiply the length of the next longest side by itself. +_____.

   Arrange that number of poker chips in four rows along that side.

3. Add these two numbers together. =_____.

Pythagoras says the sum of these two numbers will equal the length of the longest side multiplied by itself.

4. Multiply the longest side by itself.

   Longest side x longest side =_____.

5. Are the two numbers the same? _____.

   You should be able to arrange all the poker chips in five rows along the longest side.

6. How many poker chips will be in each row? _____.

3 inches

5 inches

4 inches

Medicine

The Greeks believed that illness was a punishment sent by the gods. A sick person would pray to Asclepius, the god of healing. Shrines to Asclepius were built all over the ancient Greek world. People slept in the temples and hoped that Asclepius would come to them in a dream and tell them how to cure their illness. Priests at the shrines helped to cure people by prescribing rest, herbs, and simple foods. Snakes were considered sacred in ancient Greece. A live snake was kept in all temples dedicated to Asclepius. The staff of Asclepius was entwined by a single snake and called a *caduceus*.

As well as going to a temple, people would go to the doctor. Doctors knew how to treat injuries, but not how to cure diseases. There were several schools of medicine, and each had its own ideas on the best way to treat patients. Hippocrates, the most famous Greek physician, believed that with rest and plain food, a body could cure itself.

Project
Learn about the Hippocratic Oath and design a poster.

Materials
- internet access or encyclopedias
- tagboard
- markers

Directions
1. Look at a copy of the ancient Greek Hippocratic Oath. Try to put it into your own words using modern-day language.
2. Now, find a copy of the modern version used in medicine today. How close did your version come to the modern day version? Discuss changes that have been made to the oath as a class.
3. Revise your oath if necessary and then copy the wording onto tagboard. Illustrate your poster with a caduceus.

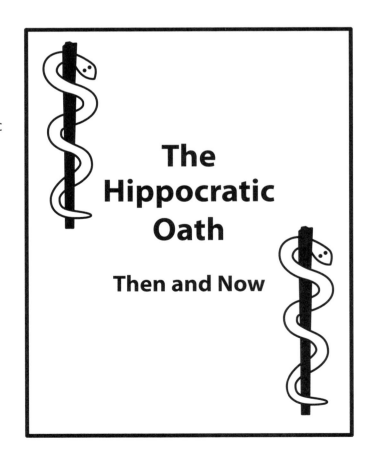

The Hippocratic Oath

Then and Now

Sports

Sports competitions were popular in all the city-states of ancient Greece. Athletes trained from the time they were children to participate in the events. Small towns held competitions, and athletes would travel from all over Greece to participate in the great sanctuaries at Olympia and Delphi.

Wrestling was a popular sport, as was *pancratium*, a combination of mud wrestling and boxing. Other favorite sports included the javelin and discus throw. A discus could weigh up to 8½ pounds (38 kg)! Probably the most popular sport of all was the foot race. Athletes would compete on a track of about 200 feet (60 meters).

The festival of the Olympic Games was held every four years in the sanctuary of Zeus. At the end of the games, which lasted for seven days, there was a procession and banquet. The winners of the events were considered heroes.

Project

Have fun pretending a Frisbee disc is an ancient Greek discus.

Materials

- Frisbee disc
- aluminum foil
- permanent marker
- targets such as traffic cones or chalk circles drawn on the pavement
- measuring tape

Directions

1. Cover Frisbee with foil. Copy Greek letters onto the "discus" with permanent marker using the illustration below as a guide.
2. Take turns throwing the "discus." See who can throw it the farthest. Another game is to try to aim the "discus" to land as close as possible to a target.

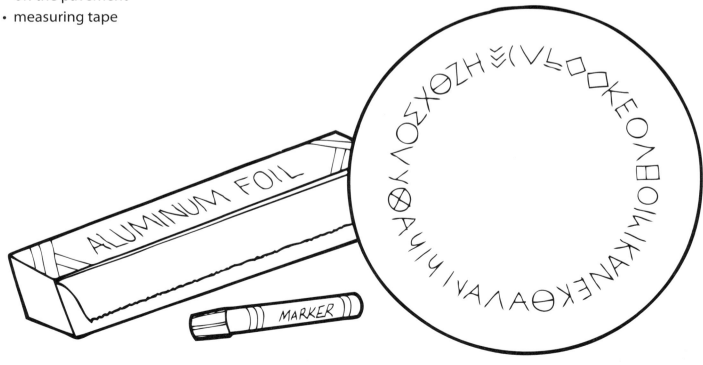

Housing

The Greeks lived in houses made of sun-dried mud bricks with thatched or tiled roofs. Houses had small windows placed high on the outside wall or none at all. The rooms opened onto a central courtyard which was the main living area of the home. Here is where the family's altar to Zeus was kept. This is also where the family ate, relaxed, and slept in good weather.

The number of rooms depended on the wealth of the family. Women had their own separate apartments called the *gynecaeum*. This area included a room where the weaving looms and yarn were kept and a room for entertaining guests. The men of the household entertained in a dining room called the *andron*. Other rooms included the kitchen, bedrooms, bathroom, and the slaves' rooms. Often, a craftsman would have his workshop in the room facing the street.

Project
Pretend to be an architect designing a Greek home.

Materials
- graph paper
- pencil
- ruler
- colored pencils

Directions
1. Using graph paper to help make straight lines, design a Greek home. Include:

   - courtyard
   - well
   - altar to Zeus
   - bedrooms
   - slaves' rooms
   - kitchen
   - men's dining room
   - women's rooms
   - weaving room
   - storage room
   - bathroom
   - craftsman's workshop

2. Add details with colored pencils.

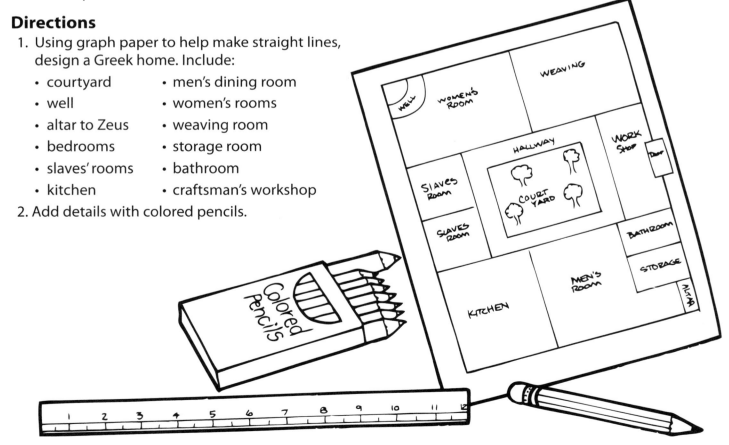

Furniture

Homes in ancient Greece were not usually decorated. The walls were whitened with lime and there was little furniture. Everything from cups to lutes was hung from nails on the walls. Blankets were stored in chests and personal possessions were kept in baskets or small boxes. Tables and chairs were made of light wood and were often inlaid with ivory, gold, or silver.

The man of the house sat on a large chair called a *thronos*. A smaller chair with curved legs was called a *klismos*. Most people sat on stools that often had folding legs. Diners reclined on cushioned couches and ate from small three-legged dining tables that could be pushed under the couch when not in use. The couches used at mealtime were similar to the ones used for sleeping. They were made of wood, often decorated with bronze, and had a base of leather cords. A fabric-covered mat of reeds was used as the upholstery.

Project

Think about the elements of design that Greek craftsmen used when building storage chests and make a small decorative box.

Materials

- shoebox or other small box
- variety of materials such as pasta shapes, dried beans, or shells

Directions

1. Think about how to best arrange the selected materials to create a pleasing design. Try to use a mixture of colors and textures.

2. Apply a layer of glue to the outside of the box. Do one small area at a time. Glue the materials onto the top and sides of the box.

3. Let dry.

Clothing

The clothing worn by the ancient Greeks was similar in shape for both men and women and changed little in design for hundreds of years.

The basic dress was a straight tunic called a *chiton* (ki´-ton). Made from a single rectangle of cloth, a chiton was cut into two pieces, pinned at intervals from the neck to the elbow and gathered at the waist with a belt. Another piece of material might be draped over the top to make a cloak called a *himation* (hi mat´e on). Workmen, soldiers, and boys wore their tunics short. Women, girls, and older men wore a longer style.

For ordinary days, brown tunics were the common attire. For more formal occasions, bleached white tunics were worn. Clothing was often edged with a colorful stripe or with a "key" pattern.

Project
Experience wearing clothing similar to that worn by the ancient Greeks.

Materials
- large pieces of fabric, solid-colored sheets, or large paper tablecloths
- scissors
- markers
- safety pins

Directions
1. Cut fabric into two lengths as long as the wearer is tall and about 36 inches (90 cm) wide. Cut additional fabric into long strips for a belt and headband.

2. Decorate the hem in a key pattern with a marker.

3. To wear: Pin the two pieces of fabric together at the shoulders and at intervals down the sleeves. Tie with a belt. Belts were worn high or at the waist depending on the current fashion. Sometimes two belts were worn with the fabric gently pulled out a bit between them.

4. Make a headpiece by tying a fabric strip around the head. Girls may wish to crisscross their headband or make a headdress from the directions on pages 32–33.

EP062 Ancient Greece © Highsmith® Inc. 2007

Festival

Each city-state had a patron god and every year the people held a festival to honor their special god or goddess.

The patron of Athens was the goddess Athena. Every summer her festival, called the *Panathenaea*, began with a relay torch race. The winner lit the sacred fire on Athena's altar. At dawn of the following day, a procession began with girls carrying cups and incense burners. Behind them came white oxen, water carriers, and musicians. A decorated cart carried a new embroidered robe called a *peplos* for Athena's statue. At the end of the procession marched the priests, officials, and townspeople. The oxen were sacrificed and roasted. The celebration continued for two days with feasting, dancing, singing, poetry competitions, and games.

Project

Have a relay torch race like the ones held by the citizens of Athens centuries ago.

Materials

- red, yellow, and orange construction paper
- paper towel tube
- aluminum foil
- scissors
- masking tape

Directions

1. Divide into teams. Each team should make a torch.
2. Wrap aluminum foil around the paper towel tube.
2. Cut the construction paper into strips as shown. One at a time, attach the strips on the masking tape as you wrap the tape around the tube. The colors should alternate.

3. Have a relay race. Spread out the team members along the racetrack. The first runner holds the torch. When the race begins, he or she runs to the next player and passes the torch. Racers continue running and passing the torch until the last player crosses the finish line. That player's team wins!

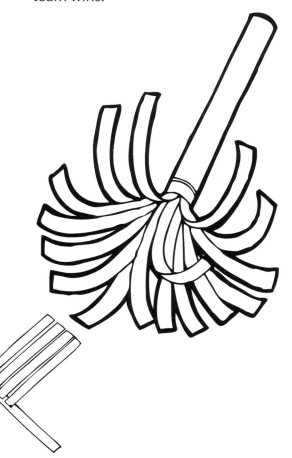

Poetry

Ancient Greek authors enjoyed writing many types of poetry. A favorite style of poetry was the epic poem. These poems are long and tell of the adventures of heroes and divine beings.

The greatest Greek poet was Homer, who wrote two famous epic poems, *The Iliad* and *The Odyssey*. *The Iliad* tells the story of the Trojan war and the heroic deeds of Greek and Trojan soldiers like Achilles and Hektor. The Odyssey continues the story with the return home of one Greek soldier named Odysseus. It took him 10 years to get home with many adventures along the way. These poems taught history, geography, and religion, as well as lessons in bravery. Schoolboys often recited from these poems at festivals.

Project

After listening to the story of the Trojan horse described in *The Iliad*, draw what you think the horse looked like.

Materials

- The Story of the Trojan Horse
- paper
- crayons or colored pencils

Directions

1. Read or listen to the story of the Trojan Horse based on the epic poem *The Iliad*, by Homer.

2. Draw a picture of what the Trojan horse might have looked like. Ask yourself these questions before beginning the design: How did the Greek soldiers get into the horse? How did they breathe? How did they get out of the horse without being heard?

For the Teacher

Read The Story of the Trojan Horse to students. Discuss.

The Story of the Trojan Horse

For 10 long years, the Greeks tried to capture the city of Troy. The soldiers became tired and wanted to return home to their families. They decided to trick the Trojans to make them surrender. They built a giant, hollow, wooden horse and filled it with soldiers. The rest of the Greek army sailed away leaving the horse behind. A Greek spy named Sinon persuaded the Trojans to take the horse into the city. He told them the horse was magic and would keep them from harm. The horse was brought into Troy, and the citizens went to bed thinking they were safe, thanks to the magical horse. During the night, however, Sinon let out the armed troops hiding in the horse. The soldiers overpowered the guards and let in the remaining Greek troops who had snuck back from the ships in the darkness. A fierce battle followed, but Troy was captured and the city burned.

EP062 Ancient Greece © Highsmith® Inc. 2007

Aesop's Fables

Aesop was a Greek slave who lived in the sixth century B.C. It is believed that he wrote a collection of fables featuring animals that talk and act like human beings. A fable is a brief tale that teaches a lesson or offers advice.

One of Aesop's most popular fables is the story of "The Tortoise and the Hare." The hare is so confident that he will win the race that he stops for a nap. The slow but steady tortoise keeps right on plodding along and not only passes the sleeping hare, but wins the race. This story teaches that persistence can be more valuable than speed.

The story of "The Ant and the Grasshopper" teaches the importance of hard work and planning ahead. When winter comes, the hard-working ant has plenty to eat, but the grasshopper, who spent the summer playing, starves.

For the Teacher

Project
Perform one of Aesop's fables in a play.

Materials
- Copies of Aesop's Fables, (obtain from your local library)

Directions
1. Divide students into groups.
2. Give groups time to read their fables. Allow each group to assign students within the group to act out the characters in the fable.
3. Groups take turns performing their plays for the other groups.

Some of Aesop's Fables
- "The Ant and the Grasshopper"
- "The Shepherd Boy and the Wolf"
- "The Dove and the Ant"
- "The Tortoise and the Hare"
- "The Lion and the Mouse"
- "The Crow and the Pitcher"

Constellations

The names given by the Greeks to the constellations are the ones we still use today. These names were based on myths such as the one about Orion.

Orion was a great hunter and often boasted about his skill. This bragging made the goddess Juno angry. One day when Orion and his dogs were hunting rabbit, Juno had a scorpion sting Orion and kill him.

The physician, Asclepius, brought Orion back to life using skills he learned from snakes. The god of the dead, Pluto, did not like the fact that the dead could be brought back to life! When he told his brother, Jupiter, of his worries, Jupiter threw his mighty thunderbolts, killing both Orion and Asclepius for good. Everyone, including the hare, the scorpion, and Asclepius' snake, was put in the sky among the stars.

Project
Identify the characters in the myth of Orion in the stars.

Materials
- Constellations page
- pencils

Directions
1. Connect the dots to find the shapes of Orion, his two dogs, the hare, the scorpion, and the physician Asclepius and his snake.

For the Teacher
Reproduce Constellations (page 29) for each student.

Constellations

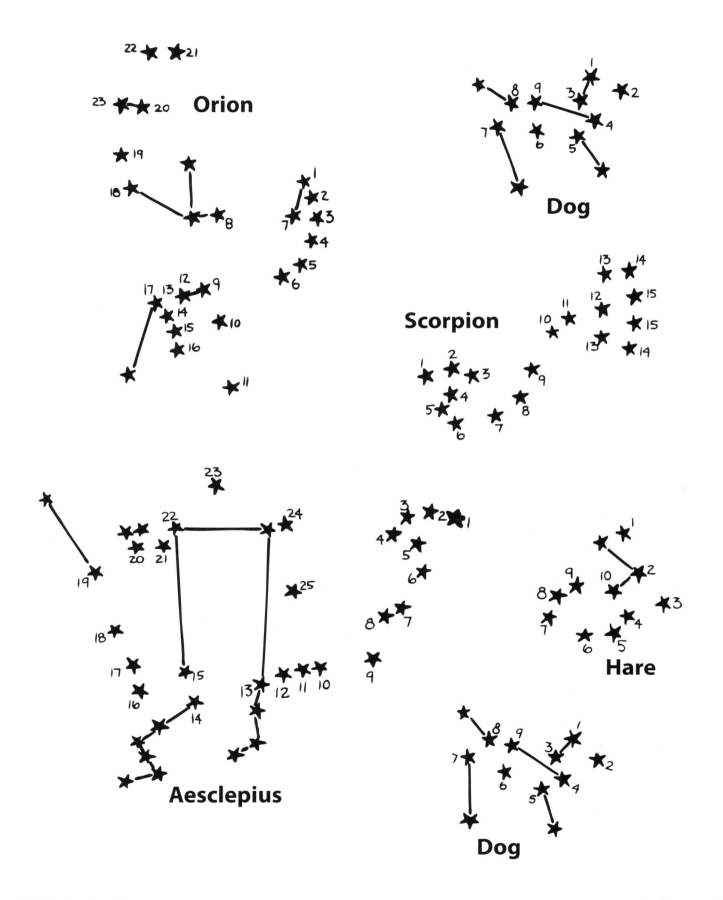

Orion

Dog

Scorpion

Aesclepius

Hare

Dog

Gods and Goddesses

The gods and goddesses worshiped by the ancient Greeks were a lot like humans: they fell in love, married, had children, and felt anger and jealousy. All gods and goddesses were descendents of Gaea (the Earth) and Uranus (the Sky). Everything that happened was willed by the gods. Zeus, the chief god, controlled the weather and Aphrodite made people fall in love. Demeter and her daughter, Persephone, were responsible for the harvest. Poseidon was ruler of the seas. Soldiers sought favor from Ares, the god of war. Athena was the goddess of wisdom, war, and the arts.

Religion played a large part in the everyday life of the Greeks. The people spent much of their time giving thanks to the gods and warding off bad fortune. Offerings of milk, wine, and cakes were made to the gods as well as animal sacrifices. Many festivals and sporting events were held to honor the gods throughout the year.

Project
Read the Myth of Arachne and write an original myth.

Materials
- The Myth of Arachne
- paper
- pen or pencil

Directions
1. Read the Greek myth of Arachne.
2. Write a story to explain some natural event. For example, the story of Arachne answers the question "Where did spiders come from?" Include mythical creatures, mortals, and heroes.

For the Teacher
Copy one Myth of Arachne (page 31) per student.

The Myth Of Arachne

Arachne was a young maiden who became a skillful weaver. She was so talented that she became quite famous. When people came to see her work, they would gaze in awe at her beautiful designs. Even the nymphs from the streams and forests would come to watch the graceful Arachne at work. Arachne's admirers would say, "The goddess Athena must have taught Arachne herself, for no mortal girl could learn such a skill on her own."

This made Arachne quite angry, as she had been taught to weave as a child by her father. Over the years, she spent many hours each day at her loom perfecting her skill. "It is through my own hard work that I have become such a wonderful weaver, not because of any help from the goddess. Besides, there is nothing that Athena could teach me, as I have become as good a weaver as Athena herself. Perhaps even better!"

One day an old woman came to watch Arachne weave. When she heard the girl's boasts, she begged her to ask forgiveness of the goddess. "Do not dare to compare yourself to the immortals," she warned Arachne, "it should be enough that you are the finest weaver among mortals."

Arachne turned to the old woman. "Why shouldn't I speak the truth," she said indignantly. "If Athena was here I would challenge her to a contest to prove that I am the most skillful weaver of all. " Upon hearing these words, the old woman threw down her cane and revealed herself to be, in fact, the goddess Athena. "I accept your challenge," said Athena as she sat down at a loom.

Although she never really thought that the goddess would hear of her boasts, Arachne took her place at her loom and the contest began. People gathered from all over to watch the weavers at work. Arachne threw the shuttle from hand to hand between the threads, but as fast as she worked, Athena was just a little faster. A picture soon formed on Athena's loom, a picture that was a last warning to Arachne to repent and ask forgiveness for her pride and boasting. When Arachne saw the goddess's work, she became even angrier! As the crowd looked on in amazement, Arachne wove her bright threads into a pattern of scenes that showed the gods as evil deceivers, who often played cruel tricks on their mortal servants.

As soon as Athena noticed what Arachne had done, she tore Arachne's work into bits. "You have insulted me and all the gods," raged Athena, "and such wickedness shall not go unpunished." Then she touched Arachne and said, "Live on and spin, and your descendents, too. Anyone who sees you will be reminded that it is not wise to anger Athena." At those words, Arachne's body began to shrivel and distort before the horrified watchers, and she was transformed into a spider. All spiders descend from Arachne. They spin and weave their fine thread and remind mortals of the foolishness of Arachne.

Headddresses

The participants at religious festivals often wore wreaths made from vines on their heads. Speakers at the Assembly in Athens wore headdresses made of myrtle when they addressed their audience. Beautiful gold wreaths decorated the heads of many of the statues of gods and goddesses. The only prize given at the Olympics was a simple wreath of wild olive leaves. Wreaths were even placed on the heads of corpses in tombs.

Wreaths were not the only type of headdress worn in ancient Greece. Hairstyles were very elaborate, and women often wore a gold or fabric headband. Elaborate crowns, called *diadems,* were made from the gold brought back from Persia by the troops of Alexander the Great. Men, too, wore headbands or golden circlets in their hair. For traveling, however, a man might wear a wide-brimmed hat called a *petasos*. It could be made of wool, fur, or straw and it protected him from the sun.

Project
Make one or more of the many types of headdresses worn by the ancient Greeks.

Materials
- tagboard
- white tissue paper
- green chenille sticks
- gold paint
- scissors
- glue
- green construction paper
- bobby pins
- paintbrushes
- aluminum foil
- Leaf and Diadem Patterns

For the Teacher
Make several sets of Leaf Patterns (page 33) on tagboard for students to trace. Make diadems as shown below. A diadem is like a tiara in that it does not go all the way around the head.

Directions
Vine Wreath
1. Trace leaf patterns many times onto construction paper and cut out.
2. Cut chenille sticks into 6-inch (15-cm) lengths. Glue a leaf to each stem. Twist two stems together. Keep adding one stem at a time to make a vine. Form the vine into a circle and twist together.
3. If making a myrtle wreath, cut tissue paper into small squares and crush to make myrtle blossoms. Glue to the myrtle wreath.

Golden Diadem
1. Get a diadem from your teacher.
2. Cut foil into long strips about 3 inches (7.5 cm) wide. Gently crush the foil and roll between the hands to make long twists. Wrap the foil twists around the front part of the diadem, keeping the twists close together. Cover the side pieces with foil.
3. Paint the foil gold and let dry. Use bobby pins to attach diadem to head.

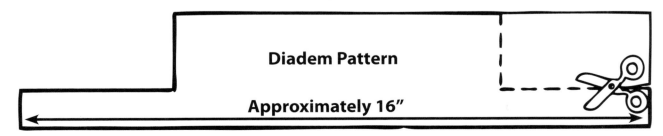

Diadem Pattern

Approximately 16"

Leaf Patterns

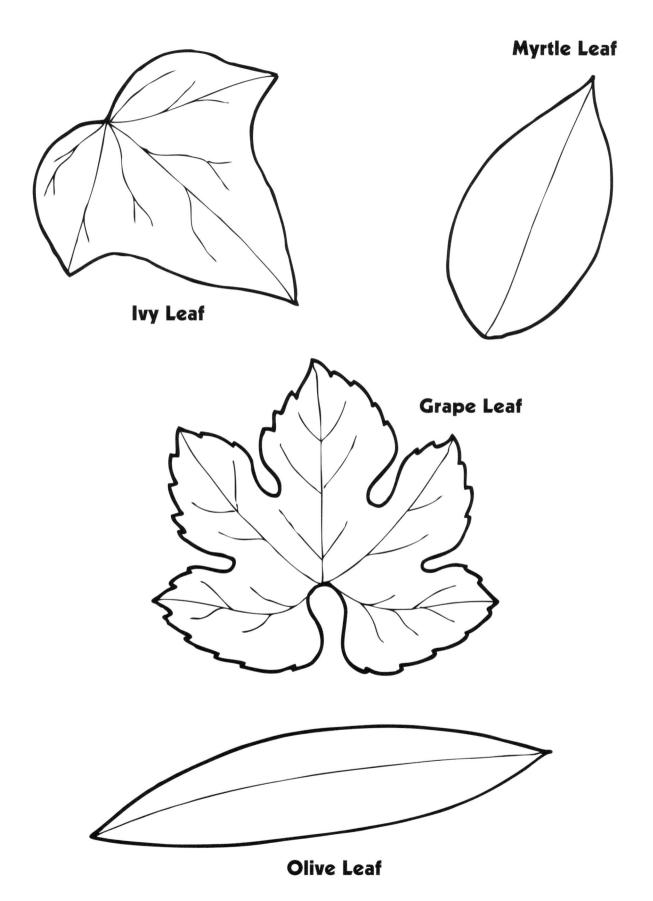

Myrtle Leaf

Ivy Leaf

Grape Leaf

Olive Leaf

Cosmetics and Perfume

Greek women enjoyed using cosmetics and perfumed oils. Perfume was imported from Corinth and Rhodes in colorful glass jars or clay pots. A woman would use a special jar called a *pyxis* to hold her powder and cosmetics. These lidded jars were round and flat and made from clay. They were often painted with domestic scenes, such as women spinning and weaving. Using cosmetics was only part of a Greek woman's skin care. Girls and women were careful to keep out of the sun because a suntan was considered unattractive.

After exercising, men would rub their bodies with oils to keep their skin supple. They would remove the excess oil with a curved bronze body scraper. Men were known to use perfumes as well. The fierce warriors of Sparta perfumed their long hair before going into battle.

Project

Make a *pyxis* or ancient Greek cosmetic jar.

Materials

- empty 12 oz. (360 ml) tuna can
- Pyxis Pattern
- scissors
- colored pencils (authentic colors would be rust, black, and light and dark beige)
- tagboard
- pencil
- glue
- tape

Directions

1. Trace the handle pattern onto tagboard. Cut out, color, and fold on dotted line.
2. Color and cut out the jar and lid patterns. Use tape to attach the two parts of the jar pattern into one long strip.
3. Wrap the jar pattern around the tuna can and tape.
4. Color and glue the lid pattern onto tagboard and trim around the edge. Carefully cut a slit in the center of the lid. Insert handle and tape the edges.

For the Teacher

Copy one Pyxis Pattern (page 35) per student.

Pyxis Pattern

Lid

Handle

Jar

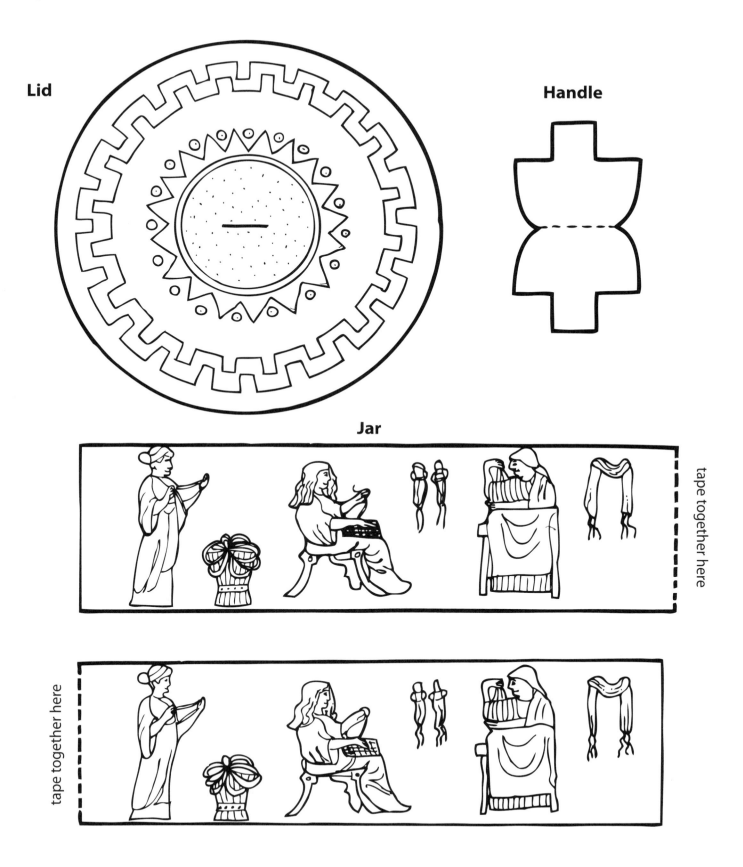

tape together here

tape together here

Jewelry

Wealthy women owned jewelry, much of it gold and silver. Many women had pierced ears and wore very ornate earrings. Jewels such as coral, agate, amber, and cornelians were often set in gold to make elaborate pins and necklaces. Bracelets made with animal heads were popular in ancient Greece and were probably worn by both men and women. Rings were often set with colorful stones and sometimes the stones were carved with tiny pictures.

Beautiful jewelry was made using the technique called *granulation*. Artists would decorate the surface of a piece of jewelry by grouping tiny granules of gold into triangles to form an intricate design. This style of jewelry was made popular by Mycenaean craftsmen in the 1300s B.C.

Project

Make a bracelet to learn about the granulation technique used by ancient craftsmen.

Materials

- tagboard
- pencil
- scissors
- glue or stapler
- tiny pasta such as egg pastina
- gold paint
- paintbrushes

Directions

1. Cut the tagboard into a strip about 3 x 8 inches (7.5 x 20 cm).

2. Draw a design of triangles onto the tagboard. Fill in the triangles with glue. Sprinkle the pastina over the glued area or arrange in rows within the triangle. Let dry. Paint with gold paint.

3. Bend into a circle. Glue or staple into a bracelet.

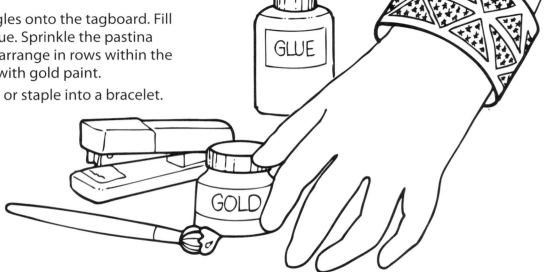

Music

Music was an important part of life in ancient Greece. Greeks sang songs at weddings, births, and funerals. The Greeks also sang many love songs, drinking songs, and songs of thanksgiving to the gods. Poetry was often recited to music. There were battle songs as well, and the music from pipes kept rowers and foot soldiers on the march in time with each other.

Greek musicians played string instruments like the harp and the lyre. The soundbox of a lyre was made from an empty tortoise shell! A *kithara* is a larger wooden version of a lyre. It was plucked with a *plectrum* which is very similar to a modern guitar pick. Cymbals and drums were popular, as well as wind instruments like the *auloi* or double pipes and the *syrinx*. Syrinx, or panpipes, were made of reeds of different lengths and were named for the nymph, Syrinx, who turned herself into a reed.

Project

Make a set of panpipes to learn about one type of instrument played in ancient Greece.

To Play: Hold the panpipes so the straws point downwards. Blow across the tops of the straws rather than into them.

Materials

- tagboard
- ruler
- colored pencils or crayons
- drinking straws
- scissors

Directions

1. Cut the tagboard into a rectangle about 2 x 10 inches (5 x 25 cm) long. Decorate one side.

2. Glue the straws onto the tagboard. Space them about 2 inches (5 cm) apart.

3. Fold the tagboard over the straws and glue. Trim the longer ends of the straws so that each one is a little shorter than the one next to it.

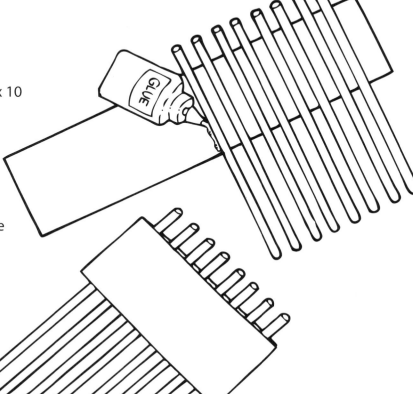

Symposia

Wealthy Greek men held banquet parties, called *symposia,* for their male friends. As the guests arrived, slaves would remove the men's sandals and bathe their feet. The evening began with a toast to Dionysus, the god of wine.

The guests sat on long couches to eat and drink. Slaves would serve dishes of bread, olives, fish or lamb, nuts, and grapes. For a special symposium, guests might enjoy oysters, snails, or doves. There were no forks, so the food was eaten with fingers.

After dinner, singing, dancing, music, sharing stories, and discussion of intellectual topics would commence. The men discussed literature, history, science, philosophy, and mathematics. They were also entertained by juggling and acrobatic shows.

For the Teacher

Project

Taste a dessert that is similar to one served at an ancient Greek symposium.

Materials

- ½ cup (120 ml) butter
- large bowl
- ⅔ cup (150 ml) honey
- big wooden spoon
- 1 cup (236.6 ml) farina (instant oatmeal)
- saucepan
- ½ tsp. (2.45 ml) ground cinnamon
- 2 eggs
- ½ cup (120 ml) ground almonds
- hot pads
- 8-inch (20 cm) square cake pan

Syrup

- measuring cups and spoons
- 1 cup (240 ml) honey
- ½ cup (120 ml) water

Directions

1. Students can grind nuts in class for an authentic experience of Greek cooking methods. It will take about 1½ cups (360 ml) shelled almonds to make ½ cup (120 ml) ground nuts. To grind nuts, you'll need a big wooden bowl and a fist-sized stone. Scrub stone thoroughly with soap before using it to break up and pulverize nuts.

2. Cream butter by beating it with spoon until fluffy and light in color. Add honey gradually, beating well after each addition. Gradually add farina, cinnamon, and nuts.

3. Place in a greased cake pan. Bake at 350° F (175° C) for 35 minutes. Cool for 15 minutes.

4. While cake is baking, make syrup by boiling honey and water together for 10 minutes. Pour over partially cooled cake. Cool cake completely.

5. Cut into diamond shapes. Makes 16 pieces.

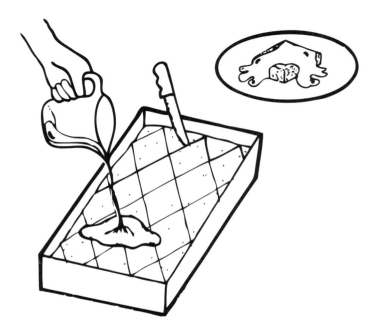

Weaving

Girls in ancient Greece did not go to school. They were taught at home by their mothers to be good homemakers. They learned to look after the house and to spin and weave. In addition, some wealthy women learned to read and write to help them keep track of the household supplies.

Weaving was practiced by all Greek women. Weaving was considered a necessary and noble art. Almost every home had a loom. In some homes, the loom was kept in the kitchen. Larger homes had an entire room set aside for the loom and yarns.

The wool from local sheep was spun into such fine thread that Greek garments were very thin. The women also wove blankets in beautiful colors. The houses had no glass in the windows so women had to make sure they had enough blankets for winter.

Project
Learn to weave on a cardboard loom.

Materials
- cardboard
- ruler
- scissors
- safety pin
- tape
- plastic fork

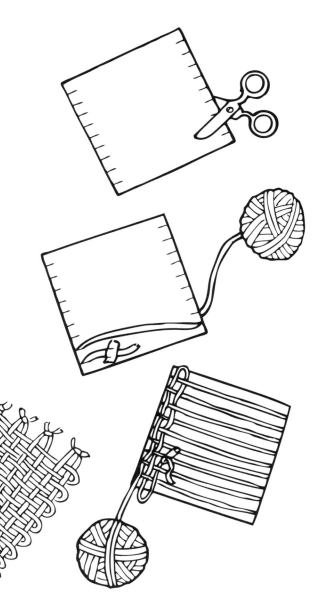

Directions
1. Cut the cardboard into a square about 8 inches (20 cm) on each side. Cut notches into the top and bottom edges.
2. Tape one end of a long strand of yarn to the back of the cardboard. Wrap yarn around cardboard feeding it into the notches as you go. These threads are called the warp threads.
3. Thread the yarn through a safety pin and tie a knot.
4. Weave yarn strands over and under the warp threads. Use a plastic fork to push the lines of weaving close together. When you finish, turn the weaving over, cut the middle of the warp threads, remove cardboard and tie off ends.

Sculpture

The Greeks created some of the greatest sculptures known. Unlike Egyptian sculptors, Greek artists created figures that were graceful and lifelike.

Gods, goddesses, and athletes were favorite subjects. Artists often sculpted their male models draped only in a cloak to make them look more noble.

A famous Greek sculptor named Pheidias was chosen to make the great statue of Athena that stood inside the Parthenon. The statue stood more than 39 feet (11.9 m) tall! Athena was carved from ivory plates affixed to a wooden frame and was dressed in a robe of gold. Her eyes were jewels and her wrists and waist were wreathed with snakes. She carried a massive shield and spear and had a giant snake at her side. On her head was a helmet crowned with golden horses.

Project
Greek sculptors were able to carve marble to look like draped fabric! Experiment with papier-mâché to make a sculpture.

Materials
- Athena Sculpture page
- newspaper
- masking tape
- tagboard
- white glue
- white muslin fabric scraps
- scissors
- tempera paint
- brushes

Directions
1. Follow the directions on the Athena Sculpture page to make a sculpture of Athena, the Greek goddess of wisdom, war, and the arts.

For the Teacher
Copy one Athena Sculpture (page 41) per student.

Athena Sculpture

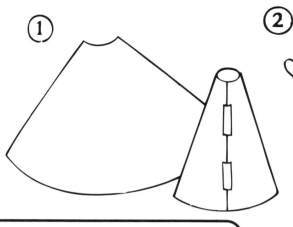

1. Cut the tagboard as shown and form into a cone. Tape closed.

2. Crush a piece of newspaper into a ball and tape to the top of the cone. Roll a half sheet of newspaper into a tight roll and bend in half. Tape to the cone to make arms.

3. Cut hand shapes from tagboard and tape to the ends of the arms.

4. Mix two parts white glue to one part water. Cut newspaper into long thin strips.

5. Dip the strips into the glue and water mixture. Run the pieces between the fingers to remove the excess glue. Lay over the form to create shoulders, the rest of the figure, and facial features. Make hair by attaching paper curls to head.

6. Cut two squares of fabric about the height of the figure. Dip in glue mixture and gently squeeze out excess. Drape over figure to form chiton (see Clothing, page 24).

7. Let dry. This may take a day or two.

8. Because Greek statues were painted, apply tempera paint to desired areas.

Pottery

The Greeks were excellent potters. Some of the finest vases and jars were made in the potters' quarters in Athens. Our word *ceramics* comes from the Greek word *keramikos*, which means "pottery." When the clay was put into the kiln and fired, it turned a reddish-brown color. The craftsmen learned that they could paint on their pots with gel made from very fine clay mixed with water. During the firing process, this clay "paint" would turn black.

Early Greek potters decorated their vases in this black-figure style. They painted the silhouettes of figures onto the pots before firing. After firing, the figures would turn black giving this style the name "black-figure technique." Soon after 500 B.C., the red-figure technique became popular. Now the figures were left on the red clay and the background was painted with the solution that turned black.

Project

Make a crayon resist of a Greek amphora, or storage jar, in the red-figure style.

Materials

- Pottery Pattern
- scissors
- red-brown or golden brown color crayon
- black watercolor paint
- paintbrush

Directions

1. Draw the outlines of a design on the jar using pencil. Scenes from favorite stories were often found on Greek containers.

2. Color in the figures and designs with the brown crayon. Press down to leave a thick layer of crayon.

3. Paint over the entire jar with black watercolor paint. The paint will only cover the paper and the figures will remain brown! Don't worry about staying in the lines.

4. Cut out the jar.

For the Teacher

Reproduce a copy of the Pottery Pattern (below) for each student. (Enlarge pattern by 175 percent.)

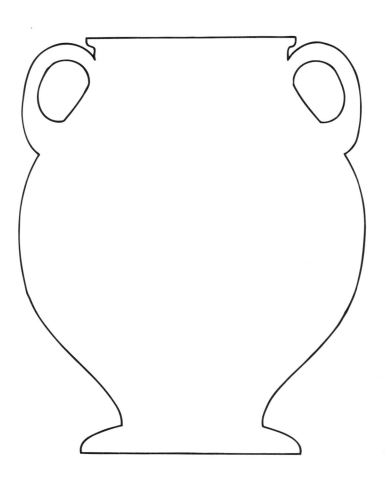

Games and Toys

If a child from ancient Greece were to join a modern class at recess, he or she would have no trouble recognizing the games being played! Greek children played on swings and enjoyed many types of ball games, including a hockey-type game played with curved sticks. Children's toys included tops, yo-yos, and soft leather balls stuffed with bran and used for juggling. Hoop games were popular, as well as hopscotch and a game similar to jacks that was played with the knucklebones from animals. Babies played with rattles, and girls played with clay dolls, some with hinged arms and legs.

Adults enjoyed game-playing as well. Soldiers would often play board games when taking a break from fighting. They played games similar to chess and backgammon. The modern game Chutes and Ladders™ is very similar to a game of snakes and ladders played in ancient times.

For the Teacher

Project

Have a game day featuring some of the games enjoyed by children of ancient Greece.

Materials

- yo-yos
- Hula-Hoops™
- chalk
- small stones
- jacks
- snakes and ladders game
- juggling balls

Directions

1. Make the game board, tops, and juggling balls on the following page or have the students bring these toys from home.
2. Set up an area for each of the games to be played.
3. Rotate the students through the stations so everyone gets a chance to play.

Hopscotch

Materials: chalk, stones, playground or sidewalk

Directions

1. Draw a hopscotch court on the pavement, as illustrated. Make each square about 1 foot square (.0929 m^2). Number squares from 1–10.
2. Each player gets one stone. The first player tosses the stone onto square #1, hops over the square landing on square #2. Only one foot can be on a square at a time and feet can't touch the lines.
3. Hop square to square to #10 and back again. Stop at square #2 and pick up stone in square #1. Hop over square #1. If successful, player continues tossing his or her stone into square #2 this time. Player continues until a toss is missed, a foot touches the line, or two feet land in a square.
4. The winner is the first one to successfully get through all numbers.

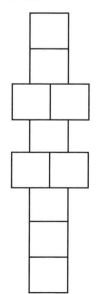

Games and Toys

Juggling Balls

Materials: fabric, scissors, needle, thread, uncooked rice or beans

Directions

1. Cut fabric into six circles.  Place two circles' right sides together. Stitch almost all the way around leaving an opening about 1 inch (2.54 cm) wide. Turn right side out. Fill with rice and stitch closed. Repeat to make a set of three.

2. Practice tossing one ball back and forth from one hand to another. Graduate to two balls. Hold one ball in each hand. Toss one ball in the air the way you practiced. When ball reaches halfway point between hands, toss the second ball. Practice a lot. When this step is mastered, add third ball and you're juggling!

Hoops

Materials: 2 Hula-Hoops™, cones, a chair or chalk to mark turning point

Directions

1. Play a relay race with hoops. The hoops children of ancient Greece played with were made of wood, but a Hula-Hoop will work just as well.

2. Form two teams.

3. Players push the hoop around the turning point and back to the next teammate. If the hoop falls over, the player must go back to the start and try again. The first team to successfully roll their hoop around the turning point and back wins.

Tops

Materials: pencils, rubber bands, wooden spools, plastic lids, jar lids, cardboard circles, nails

Directions

1. Experiment with different materials to make a spinning top.

2. A pencil pushed through an empty sewing spool or a plastic lid can be made to spin. Hold the lid or spool in place with rubber bands and adjust the height on the pencil to get a good spin.

Snakes and Ladders

Materials: tagboard, ruler, pencil, crayons, markers or colored pencils, dice, buttons or bottle caps to use as markers

Directions

1. Cut tagboard into a 12-inch (30-cm) square. Draw a 1-inch (2.54-cm) border around the game board. Mark inner area into 1-inch (2.54-cm) blocks. Draw snakes and ladders as illustrated. Color and label the START and FINISH squares.

2. To play: First player rolls dice and moves that number of squares. Those who land on a ladder, move up the ladder to the square at the top of the ladder. When landing on a snake, player slides down to the square at the end of the snake. The winner is the first player to reach the finish.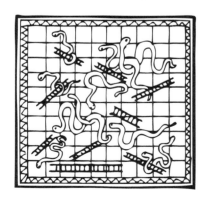

EP062 Ancient Greece © Highsmith® Inc. 2007

Food

The Greeks ate simply. Breakfast and lunch were light meals of bread dipped in wine and water followed by dried figs, olives, and perhaps some goat's milk cheese. The main meal of the day was eaten in the late afternoon or early evening and was often a barley porridge and some vegetables such as cabbage, peas, carrots, or onions. Food was eaten raw, boiled, or roasted. Bay leaves, garlic, and oregano provided the seasoning. A wealthy family's main meal might also include fish, nuts, and cheese in honey. People seldom ate meat except at religious festivals. Honey was the only sweetener available.

The Greeks were excellent bakers and made a variety of different kinds of breads, rolls, and sweets. They were the first to put unusual flavorings and seeds, such as poppy and sesame seeds, into their breads. The Greeks are credited with making the first toast!

For the Teacher

Project
Prepare and serve a typical dinner enjoyed in ancient Greece.

Materials
- ingredients for recipes, (page 46)
- knives
- cutting boards
- napkins
- measuring cups, spoons
- cups
- large bowls
- grape juice
- large spoons
- nut crackers
- plates, silverware
- hot pads

Directions
1. Bread needs to be made ahead or pita bread can be substituted.
2. Assign students to make the stew, prepare the salad, and set up the buffet.
3. Set up the buffet by pushing several desks together and cover with tablecloth. Arrange vegetables in a bowl or a terra cotta saucer for the centerpiece. For dessert, serve an assortment of walnuts, almonds, dates, apples, grapes, and figs arranged on serving dishes or terra-cotta saucers. Set out plates, silverware, and cups. Pour juice.

Decorations: (optional)
- brightly colored tablecloth
- assortment of vegetables enjoyed in ancient Greece such as parsnips, cabbage, lettuce, carrots, onions, garlic
- terra-cotta serving dishes (planter saucers work well)

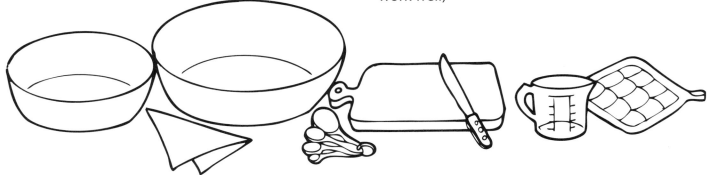

Greek Recipes

Barley Stew

- ¼ cup (60 ml) olive oil
- 2 cups (480 ml) pearl barley
- 1 large onion, minced
- 1 clove garlic, minced
- 1 cup (240 ml) chopped carrots
- 1 cup chopped celery
- 6 cups (1440 ml) boiling chicken broth
- large spoon
- electric skillet

Preparation

Heat oil in electric skillet. Sauté barley, onion, garlic, carrots, and celery in olive oil for a few minutes. Add chicken broth and cover. Cook over lowest possible heat for 25 to 45 minutes until barley has absorbed broth.

Greek Salad

- onion, sliced very thin and separated into rings
- cabbage, shredded as for coleslaw
- oregano, whole and crushed by hand, if possible
- Greek olives
- olive oil
- feta cheese
- large bowl
- mixing spoons

Preparation

Combine onion, cheese, olives, shredded cabbage, and oregano in a large bowl. Toss with olive oil. This salad can be made ahead and marinated for about one hour.

Sesame Seed Bread

- 1 cup (240 ml) lukewarm water
- 1 cup lukewarm milk
- 2 envelopes fast-acting dry yeast
- 2 Tbsp. (30 ml) sugar
- 2 Tbsp. (30 ml) oil
- 8½ cups (2040 ml) flour
- 1 tsp. (5 ml) salt
- ¼ cup (60 ml) milk
- ½ cup (120 ml) sesame seeds
- cornmeal
- electric mixer
- large bowl
- cookie sheets
- large spoon

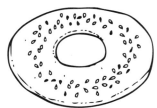

Preparation

1. Mix water and milk in a bowl. Sprinkle yeast on top and dissolve.
2. Add sugar, oil, salt, and 3 cups (720 ml) flour. Beat with electric mixer on high for 10 minutes. Stir in remaining flour.
3. Turn out onto lightly floured surface and knead for 10 minutes.
4. Cover with a large inverted metal bowl and let rise until double. Punch down. Allow to rise a second time and punch down.
5. Divide dough in half. Form dough into two doughnut shapes about 13 inches (33 cm) across. Place on a cookie sheet that has been sprinkled with cornmeal. Brush tops of loaves with milk and sprinkle with sesame seeds. Bake at 400° F (200° C) for 25–30 minutes until lightly browned.

Literature List

Ask your librarian to recommend other books about Ancient Greece.

Aesop's Fables
by Lisbeth Zwerger. North-South, 2006, reissue. 32 p. Gr. 3–6
This reissue of Lisbeth Zwerger's gorgeously illustrated edition features 12 Aesop favorites, from "The Fox and the Grapes" to "The Milkmaid and Her Pail."

Ancient Crete
by Sheldon Oberman. Crocodile Books, 2004. 103 p. Gr. 4–6
Striking illustrations complement skillful retellings of Greek myths that relate to the island of Crete and ancient Minoan civilization.

The Best Book of Ancient Greece
by Belinda Weber. Kingfisher, 2005. 32 p. Gr. 3–5
This book journeys into the realm of Zeus's mythical world as well as the everyday lives of Greece's great thinkers, citizens, and slaves.

Cultures of the World: Greece
by Jill DuBois. Benchmark Books, 2003. 2nd ed. 143 p. Gr. 5–6
Introduces the geography, history, economics, culture and people of the Mediterranean country of Greece.

Good Times Travel Agency: Adventures in Ancient Greece
by Linda Bailey. Kids Can Press, 2002. 48 p. Gr. 3–6
The Binkerton kids find themselves in ancient Greece when they travel to see the Olympic Games. Humorous illustrations and brief text show daily life, the role of women, etc.

The Hero and the Minotaur
by Robert Byrd. Dutton Children's Books, 2005. 40 p. Gr. 3–6
Join Theseus as he solves the mystery of his birth, vanquishes a colorful cast of robbers, and volunteers to slay the frightful Minotaur devouring the children of Athens.

Island of the Minotaur: Greek Myths of The Lightning Thief
by Rick Riordan. Hyperion Books for Children, 2005. 377 p. Gr. 5–8
After learning that he is the son of a mortal woman and Poseidon, god of the sea, 12-year-old Percy is sent to a summer camp for demigods like himself, and joins his new friends on a quest to prevent a war between the gods.

Jason and the Gorgon's Blood
by Jane Yolen. HarperCollins, 2004. 246 p. Gr. 4–6
Jason, who will grow up to become the head of the Argonauts, leads five other boys on a dangerous quest to save the kingdom of Iolcus, learning along the way what it means to be in command.

Myth-o-Mania: Stop That Bull, Theseus!
by Kate McMullan. Volo, 2003. 176 p. Gr. 3–6
Hades, King of the Underworld, tells the true story behind the Greek myth of Theseus, who must find his way through the labyrinth to slay the Minotaur.

The Palace of Minos at Knossos
by Christopher Scarre. Oxford University Press, 2003. 47 p. Gr. 4–6
Discusses the ancient Minoan civilization of Knossos, Crete, as shown by the excavations of that city by the archaeologist Sir Arthur Evans.

You Wouldn't Want to Be a Greek Athlete: Races You'd Rather Not Run
by Michael Ford. Franklin Watts, 2004. 32 p. Gr. 3–5
Cartoon-style introduction to the history of the Olympics.

Glossary

abacus—a frame with strings or grooves fitted with beads that slide for counting

agora—marketplace or town center

amphora—two-handled, narrow-necked pottery jar

andron—a dining room where men of the house entertained guests

Archimedes—great mathematician, engineer, and physicist of ancient times; invented Archimedean Screw, a water-removing device still used in Egypt

aulos—a flute-type instrument

bartering—trading goods and services without money

boustrophedron—writing left to right until the end of a line and then coming back from right to left on the next line; meaning "turning like an ox plowing a field"

caduceus—staff with two serpents twined around it; symbol of the medical profession

chiton—tunic worn by both men and women

city-states—small independent states consisting of a town and the surrounding farmland

clepsydra—a water clock for measuring time

diadem—an elaborate crown

ecclesia—political assembly of the citizens

Euclid—a mathematician who wrote *Elements,* which remains the basis for courses in geometry

granulation—a method of decorating jewelry involving decorating the surface of a piece of jewelry by grouping tiny granules of gold into triangles to form an intricate design

greaves—protective leg coverings for soldiers

gynecaeum—separate apartments for women

Helios—Greek sun god

Herodotus—first Greek historian; known as "The Father of History"

hoplites—foot soldiers

hoplon—large round shield carried by soldiers

keramikos—pottery

kithara—wooden version of a lyre

klismos—chair with curved legs

lyre—stringed instrument

obol—early Greek money

ostracism—banishment or exclusion from a group

Panathenaea—a festival to honor the patron of Athens, the goddess Athena.

pancratium—a combination of mud wrestling and boxing

peplos—long embroidered robe

petasos—wide-brimmed hat

phalanx—rectangular military formation

Pythagoras—mathematician who lived during the sixth century B.C. who developed many mathematical theories including the *Pythagorean Theorem,* the relationship of the sides of a right triangle

pyxis—small cosmetic jar

Sophist—professional teacher

stylus—sharp, pointed writing tool

symposium—an all-male party

syrinx—reed-type instrument

thronos—large chair used by man of the house

trireme—fast-moving warship used for ramming enemy ships